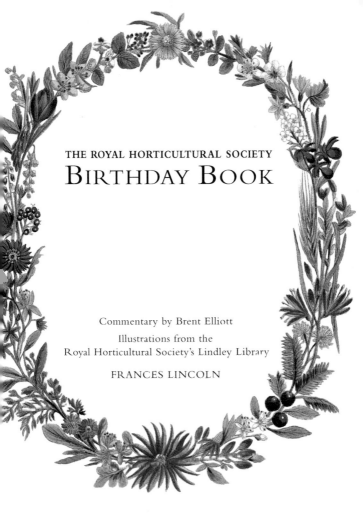

THE ROYAL HORTICULTURAL SOCIETY
BIRTHDAY BOOK

Commentary by Brent Elliott

Illustrations from the
Royal Horticultural Society's Lindley Library

FRANCES LINCOLN

Frances Lincoln Limited
4 Torriano Mews
Torriano Avenue
London NW5 2RZ
www.franceslincoln.com

The Royal Horticultural Society Birthday Book

British Library cataloguing-in-publication data
A catalogue record for this book is available from the British Library

ISBN 13: 978-0-7112-2790-3

Printed in China

First Frances Lincoln edition 2003

FRONT COVER
A hand-coloured engraving of the Surinam quassia wood, *Quassia amara*, drawn and engraved by James Sowerby, from the second volume of William Woodville's *Medical Botany* (1792)

BACK COVER
A hand-coloured engraving of *Tulipa gesneriana*, from the tenth volume of Ferdinand Vietz's *Icones Plantarum* (1819)

TITLE PAGE
A hand-coloured engraving of plants including crocus, centaurium, calendula and chicory, all contained in the first volume of Ferdinand Vietz's *Icones Plantarum* (1800), for which this was the title page illustration

OVERLEAF, RIGHT
A hand-coloured engraving of the musk mallow, *Malva moschata*, from the eighth volume of Ferdinand Vietz's *Icones Plantarum* (1818)

INTRODUCTION

The Renaissance tradition of the herbal died out in the eighteenth century, to be replaced by books on medical botany, often compiled by physicians rather than botanists. Plants were chosen on the basis of their role in *materia medica* (medicinal substances, whether animal, vegetable or mineral, used in the treatment of disease). These substances were usually dried specimens or crushed or powdered extracts, from which infusions could be prepared. Training in *materia medica* was part of a doctor's normal education and the larger hospitals often had their own gardens for growing the plants a physician would need to use. The illustrations in this book are taken from two such books on medical botany by William Woodville and Ferdinand Vietz.

William Woodville (1752–1805) became physician to the Smallpox Hospital at Battle Bridge in 1791. Here he created a two-acre garden of medicinal plants within the grounds of the hospital, which was later swept away by the development of King's Cross station. From 1790 to 1793 he published his *Medical Botany* in three volumes (with a supplement in 1794), in which he described all the plants in the *materia medica* catalogues of the Royal Colleges of Physicians. The plates are unsigned, but his prospectus indicates that James Sowerby (1757–1822), a prominent botanical artist, both drew and engraved them. A second edition appeared in 1810, and in 1832 William Jackson Hooker, later the first Director of the Royal Botanic Gardens, Kew, revised the work for a third edition. It remained the standard English work on the subject until the 1870s.

Ferdinand Bernhard Vietz (1772–1815) was Professor of Medicine at the University of Vienna from 1801 to 1812 and then Director of the University Veterinary School until his death. His major work bore the cumbersome title of *Icones Plantarum Medico-Oeconomico-Technologicarum* (pictures of medical, economic and industrial plants). The first two volumes appeared in 1800 and 1804, with the plants arranged alphabetically. He then began to work more systematically, and in 1806 issued the first of several further volumes to include plants which had not appeared in volumes one and two. This third volume incorporated plants listed alphabetically, from *Acanthus* to *Amygdalus*. After Vietz's death, Joseph L. Kerndl undertook the task of editing the remaining unpublished work. The materials must have been fairly well advanced because volumes four to ten (*Anacardium* to *Zostera*) appeared in three years, from 1817 to 1819. Finally, in 1822, Kerndl issued an eleventh, supplementary volume with a further 100 plates.

Altogether, including the supplementary volume, Vietz's work included 1035 engravings. The artist and engraver was Ignaz Albrecht or Alberti, a Viennese artist whose dates are usually given as *fl.*1780–1801, on the basis of his entry in the great German dictionary of artists by Thieme and Becker, who concluded from the lack of references to him after 1801 that he must have died about then. However it seems likely that Vietz would have commissioned additional illustrations after the first two volumes were published and the order of plates suggests that they could not have been completed until well after 1804; and there is no evidence that other artists were involved in *Icones Plantarum*.

Brent Elliott
The Royal Horticultural Society

January

1

2

3

4

5

6

7

A hand-coloured engraving of the Christmas rose,
Helleborus niger, drawn and engraved by James Sowerby,
from the first volume of William Woodville's *Medical Botany* (1790)

January

8

9

10

11

12

13

14

A hand-coloured engraving of the Seville orange, *Citrus aurantium*, from the first volume of Ferdinand Vietz's *Icones Plantarum* (1800)

January

15

16

17

18

19

20

21

A hand-coloured engraving of the saffron crocus,
Crocus sativus, drawn and engraved by James Sowerby,
from the third volume of William Woodville's *Medical Botany* (1793)

January

22

23

24

25

26

27

28

A hand-coloured engraving of the almond, *Prunus dulcis*
(formerly *Amygdalus communis*), drawn and engraved by James Sowerby,
from the second volume of William Woodville's *Medical Botany* (1792)

January ◊ *February*

29 ——————————————————————

30 ——————————————————————

31 ——————————————————————

1 ——————————————————————

2 ——————————————————————

3 ——————————————————————

4 ——————————————————————

A hand-coloured engraving of the oxlip, *Primula elatior*,
from the ninth volume of Ferdinand Vietz's *Icones Plantarum* (1819)

February

5

6

7

8

9

10

11

A hand-coloured engraving of the pineapple, *Ananas comosus* (formerly *Bromelia ananas*), from the fourth volume of Ferdinand Vietz's *Icones Plantarum* (1817)

February

12

13

14

15

16

17

18

A hand-coloured engraving of the snakeshead fritillary, *Fritillaria meleagris*, from the sixth volume of Ferdinand Vietz's *Icones Plantarum* (1817)

February

19

20

21

22

23

24

25

A hand-coloured engraving of the quince, *Cydonia oblonga*,
from the first volume of Ferdinand Vietz's *Icones Plantarum* (1800)

February ◊ March

26

27

28

29

1

2

3

A chromolithograph of the whitebeam, *Sorbus aria*,
from the fifth volume of Ferdinand Vietz's *Icones Plantarum* (1817),
where it was depicted under the name *Crataegus aria*

March

4

5

6

7

8

9

10

A hand-coloured engraving of the sweet violet,
Viola odorata, drawn and engraved by James Sowerby,
from the second volume of William Woodville's *Medical Botany* (1792)

March

11 _____

12 _____

13 _____

14 _____

15 _____

16 _____

17 _____

_____

A hand-coloured engraving of the quince, *Cydonia oblonga*,
drawn and engraved by James Sowerby, from the second volume of
William Woodville's *Medical Botany* (1792)

March

———————————————————————— 18

———————————————————————— 19

———————————————————————— 20

———————————————————————— 21

———————————————————————— 22

———————————————————————— 23

———————————————————————— 24

A hand-coloured engraving of *Hepatica nobilis* (formerly *Anemone hepatica*), from the fourth volume of Ferdinand Vietz's *Icones Plantarum* (1817)

March

25 ⎯⎯⎯⎯⎯⎯⎯⎯⎯⎯⎯⎯⎯⎯⎯⎯⎯⎯⎯⎯⎯⎯⎯⎯⎯⎯⎯⎯⎯⎯⎯⎯⎯⎯

26 ⎯⎯⎯⎯⎯⎯⎯⎯⎯⎯⎯⎯⎯⎯⎯⎯⎯⎯⎯⎯⎯⎯⎯⎯⎯⎯⎯⎯⎯⎯⎯⎯⎯⎯

27 ⎯⎯⎯⎯⎯⎯⎯⎯⎯⎯⎯⎯⎯⎯⎯⎯⎯⎯⎯⎯⎯⎯⎯⎯⎯⎯⎯⎯⎯⎯⎯⎯⎯⎯

28 ⎯⎯⎯⎯⎯⎯⎯⎯⎯⎯⎯⎯⎯⎯⎯⎯⎯⎯⎯⎯⎯⎯⎯⎯⎯⎯⎯⎯⎯⎯⎯⎯⎯⎯

29 ⎯⎯⎯⎯⎯⎯⎯⎯⎯⎯⎯⎯⎯⎯⎯⎯⎯⎯⎯⎯⎯⎯⎯⎯⎯⎯⎯⎯⎯⎯⎯⎯⎯⎯

30 ⎯⎯⎯⎯⎯⎯⎯⎯⎯⎯⎯⎯⎯⎯⎯⎯⎯⎯⎯⎯⎯⎯⎯⎯⎯⎯⎯⎯⎯⎯⎯⎯⎯⎯

31 ⎯⎯⎯⎯⎯⎯⎯⎯⎯⎯⎯⎯⎯⎯⎯⎯⎯⎯⎯⎯⎯⎯⎯⎯⎯⎯⎯⎯⎯⎯⎯⎯⎯⎯

A hand-coloured engraving of the white or Madonna lily, *Lilium candidum*, drawn and engraved by James Sowerby, from the second volume of William Woodville's *Medical Botany* (1792)

April

——————————————————— 1

——————————————————— 2

——————————————————— 3

——————————————————— 4

——————————————————— 5

——————————————————— 6

——————————————————— 7

A hand-coloured engraving of the lilac, *Syringa vulgaris*,
from the tenth volume of Ferdinand Vietz's *Icones Plantarum* (1819)

April

8 ——————————————————————

9 ——————————————————————

10 —————————————————————

11 —————————————————————

12 —————————————————————

13 —————————————————————

14 —————————————————————

A hand-coloured engraving of *Tulipa gesneriana*
from the tenth volume of Ferdinand Vietz's *Icones Plantarum* (1819)

April

15

16

17

18

19

20

21

A hand-coloured engraving of the dandelion, *Taraxacum officinale*, drawn and engraved by James Sowerby, from the first volume of William Woodville's *Medical Botany* (1790)

April

22

23

24

25

26

27

28

A hand-coloured engraving of the flag iris, *Iris germanica*,
from the seventh volume of Ferdinand Vietz's *Icones Plantarum* (1818)

April ◊ May

————————————————————————— 29

————————————————————————— 30

————————————————————————— 1

————————————————————————— 2

————————————————————————— 3

————————————————————————— 4

————————————————————————— 5

A hand-coloured engraving of the opium poppy, *Papaver rhoeas*,
from the eighth volume of Ferdinand Vietz's *Icones Plantarum* (1818)

May

6

7

8

9

10

11

12

A hand-coloured engraving of *Rosa centifolia*,
drawn and engraved by James Sowerby, from the third volume of
William Woodville's *Medical Botany* (1793)

May

13

14

15

16

17

18

19

A hand-coloured engraving of the flag iris, *Iris florentina*,
drawn and engraved by James Sowerby, from the first volume of
William Woodville's *Medical Botany* (1790)

May

20 _____

21 _____

22 _____

23 _____

24 _____

25 _____

26 _____

A hand-coloured engraving of a clove pink, *Dianthus caryophyllus*,
drawn and engraved by James Sowerby, from the second volume of
William Woodville's *Medical Botany* (1792)

May ◊ June

27

28

29

30

31

1

2

A hand-coloured engraving of the mountain laurel, *Kalmia latifolia*, from the seventh volume of Ferdinand Vietz's *Icones Plantarum* (1818)

June

3 _____

4 _____

5 _____

6 _____

7 _____

8 _____

9 _____

_____

A hand-coloured engraving of the stavesacre, *Delphinium staphisagria*, drawn and engraved by James Sowerby, from the third volume of William Woodville's *Medical Botany* (1793)

June

10

11

12

13

14

15

16

A hand-coloured engraving of *Fragaria chiloensis*,
from the sixth volume of Ferdinand Vietz's *Icones Plantarum* (1817)

June

17

18

19

20

21

22

23

A hand-coloured engraving of chicory, *Cichorium intybus*, from the second volume of Ferdinand Vietz's *Icones Plantarum* (1804)

June

24

25

26

27

28

29

30

A hand-coloured engraving of the rock-rose, *Cistus creticus*,
drawn and engraved by James Sowerby, from the second volume of
William Woodville's *Medical Botany* (1792)

July

1 _____

2 _____

3 _____

4 _____

5 _____

6 _____

7 _____

_____

A hand-coloured engraving of *Angelica sativa* (now *Angelica archangelica*), from the first volume of Ferdinand Vietz's *Icones Plantarum* (1800)

July

8

9

10

11

12

13

14

A hand-coloured engraving of a cultivated aconite or wolfsbane,
Aconitum × *cammarum*, from the third volume of
Ferdinand Vietz's *Icones Plantarum* (1806)

July

15

16

17

18

19

20

21

A hand-coloured engraving of dittany, *Dictamnus albus*,
from the first volume of Ferdinand Vietz's *Icones Plantarum* (1800)

July

22

23

24

25

26

27

28

A hand-coloured engraving of the redcurrant, *Ribes rubrum*,
drawn and engraved by James Sowerby, from the second volume of
William Woodville's *Medical Botany* (1792)

July ◊ August

29

30

31

1

2

3

4

A hand-coloured engraving of the jalap, *Ipomoea purga*, drawn and engraved by James Sowerby, from the first volume of William Woodville's *Medical Botany* (1790), where it was depicted under the name *Convolvulus jalapa*

August

———————————————————————————— 5

———————————————————————————— 6

———————————————————————————— 7

———————————————————————————— 8

———————————————————————————— 9

———————————————————————————— 10

———————————————————————————— 11

A hand-coloured engraving of the sunflower, *Helianthus annuus*,
from the seventh volume of Ferdinand Vietz's *Icones Plantarum* (1818)

August

12

13

14

15

16

17

18

A hand-coloured engraving of the common mallow, *Malva sylvestris*, drawn and engraved by James Sowerby, from the first volume of William Woodville's *Medical Botany* (1790)

August

19

20

21

22

23

24

25

A hand-coloured engraving of dittany, *Origanum dictamnus*,
from the eighth volume of Ferdinand Vietz's *Icones Plantarum* (1818)

August ◊ September

26

27

28

29

30

31

1

A hand-coloured engraving of the cardoon, *Cynara cardunculus*,
from the sixth volume of Ferdinand Vietz's *Icones Plantarum* (1817)

September

9

10

11

12

13

14

15

A hand-coloured engraving of the Turk's cap lily, *Lilium martagon*, from the seventh volume of Ferdinand Vietz's *Icones Plantarum* (1818)

September

16

17

18

19

20

21

22

A hand-coloured engraving of a cone flower, *Echinacea purpurea*, from the ninth volume of Ferdinand Vietz's *Icones Plantarum* (1819)

September

23

24

25

26

27

28

29

A hand-coloured engraving of the common mulberry, *Morus nigra*,
drawn and engraved by James Sowerby, from the second volume of
William Woodville's *Medical Botany* (1792)

30

1

2

3

4

5

6

A hand-coloured engraving of hortensia, *Hydrangea macrophylla*,
from the eleventh or supplementary volume of
Ferdinand Vietz's *Icones Plantarum* (1822)

October

7

8

9

10

11

12

13

A hand-coloured engraving of purslane, *Portulaca oleracea*,
from the ninth volume of Ferdinand Vietz's *Icones Plantarum* (1819)

October

14

15

16

17

18

19

20

A hand-coloured engraving of the common grape, *Vitis vinifera*,
from the tenth volume of Ferdinand Vietz's *Icones Plantarum* (1819)

October

21 _____

22 _____

23 _____

24 _____

25 _____

26 _____

27 _____

_____

A hand-coloured engraving of the nasturtium,
Tropaeolum majus, from the supplementary volume of
William Woodville's *Medical Botany* (1794)

October ◊ November

28

29

30

31

1

2

3

A hand-coloured engraving of the China aster, *Callistephus* (formerly *Aster*) *chinensis*, from the fourth volume of Ferdinand Vietz's *Icones Plantarum* (1817)

November

4

5

6

7

8

9

10

A hand-coloured engraving of anise, *Pimpinella anisum*,
from the first volume of Ferdinand Vietz's *Icones Plantarum* (1800)

November

11

12

13

14

15

16

17

A hand-coloured engraving of sugar cane, *Saccharum officinarum*, drawn and engraved by James Sowerby, from the third volume of William Woodville's *Medical Botany* (1793)

November

18

19

20

21

22

23

24

A hand-coloured engraving of the trumpet vine, *Campsis radicans*,
from the fourth volume of Ferdinand Vietz's *Icones Plantarum* (1817),
where it was depicted under the name *Bignonia radicans*

November ◊ December

25

26

27

28

29

30

1

A hand-coloured engraving of the pear, *Pyrus communis*,
from the ninth volume of Ferdinand Vietz's *Icones Plantarum* (1819)

December

2 _____

3 _____

4 _____

5 _____

6 _____

7 _____

8 _____

_____

A hand-coloured engraving of bergamot, *Monarda didyma*,
from the eleventh or supplementary volume of
Ferdinand Vietz's *Icones Plantarum* (1822)

December

9

10

11

12

13

14

15

A hand-coloured engraving of capers, *Capparis spinosa*,
from the fifth volume of Ferdinand Vietz's *Icones Plantarum* (1817)

December

16 _____

17 _____

18 _____

19 _____

20 _____

21 _____

22 _____

_____

A hand-coloured engraving of the Surinam quassia wood, *Quassia amara*, drawn and engraved by James Sowerby, from the second volume of William Woodville's *Medical Botany* (1792)

December

23

24

25

26

27

28

29

A hand-coloured engraving of mistletoe, *Viscum album*,
from the tenth volume of Ferdinand Vietz's *Icones Plantarum* (1819)

December

30 _____

31 _____

_____

A hand-coloured engraving of a daylily, *Hemerocallis fulva*,
from the seventh volume of Ferdinand Vietz's *Icones Plantarum* (1818)

Notes

September

2

3

4

5

6

7

8

A hand-coloured engraving of a species of St John's wort, *Hypericum perforatum*, from the first volume of Ferdinand Vietz's *Icones Plantarum* (1800)